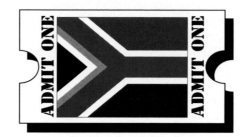

Zulu Grass Hut
With Painted
Door

FACES
AND
PLACES

SOUTH AFRICA

0 3805 01019 610

BY PATRICK RYAN

THE CHILD'S WORLD®

Country Facts

Area: 471,000 square miles.
That is about two times the size of Texas.

Population: About 45 million people.

Capital Cities: Pretoria, Cape Town, and Bloemfontein.

Other Important Cities: Johannesburg, Soweto, and Durban.

Money: The rand. One rand is divided into 100 cents.

National Language: Afrikaans and English. Many people also speak the language of their tribe.

National Songs: "Nkosi Sikeleli Afrika" and "The Call of South Africa."

National Holiday: Freedom Day on April 27.

National Flag: Red, yellow, white, green, blue, and black. The way the colors are placed on the flag have a very special meaning. All of the colors join into a single stripe. The stripe reminds the people of South Africa to work as a team.

National Motto: "Unity Is Strength."

Text copyright © 1998 by The Child's World®, Inc.
All rights reserved. No part of this book may be reproduced or utilized in any form or by any means without written permission from the publisher.
Printed in the United States of America.

Library of Congress Cataloging-in-Publication Data
Ryan, Pat (Patrick M.).
South Africa / by Pat Ryan.
Series: "Faces and Places".
p. cm.
Includes index.
Summary: Describes the geography, history, people, and customs of South Africa.
ISBN 1-56766-373-7 (hard cover, library bound)

1. South Africa — Juvenile literature. [1. South Africa.] I. Title.

DT1719.R92 1998
968 — dc20
96-30664
CIP
AC

GRAPHIC DESIGN
Robert A. Honey, Seattle

PHOTO RESEARCH
James R. Rothaus / James R. Rothaus & Associates

ELECTRONIC PRE–PRESS PRODUCTION
Robert E. Bonaker / Graphic Design & Consulting Co.

PHOTOGRAPHY
Cover photo: A group of African schoolchildren huddle together by Guy Stubbs; ABPL/Corbis

Table
of
Contents

CHAPTER	PAGE

Where Is South Africa?

Imagine that you could float high up in the air. If you looked down at the Earth, you would notice that the world has many land areas that are surrounded by water. These land areas are called continents. If you could look more closely, you would see that many of the continents are made up of several different countries.

Western Hemisphere

Eastern Hemisphere

South Africa (white) is in the east and U.S.A. (green) is in the west

South Africa is a beautiful country on the continent of Africa.

It has green grasslands, towering mountains, and hot desert.

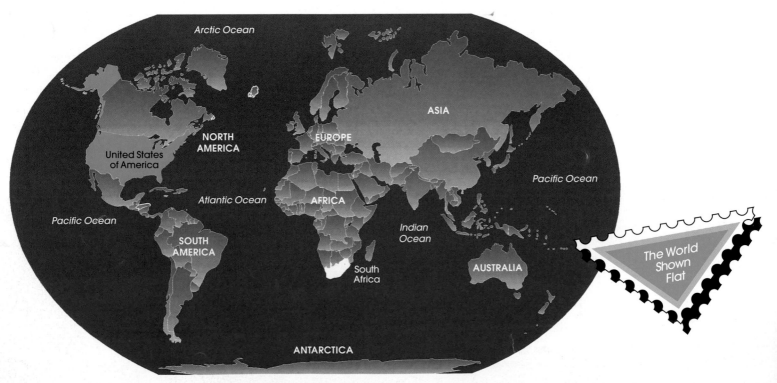

Arctic Ocean

ASIA

NORTH AMERICA

EUROPE

United States of America

Pacific Ocean

Atlantic Ocean

AFRICA

Indian Ocean

Pacific Ocean

SOUTH AMERICA

South Africa

AUSTRALIA

The World Shown Flat

ANTARCTICA

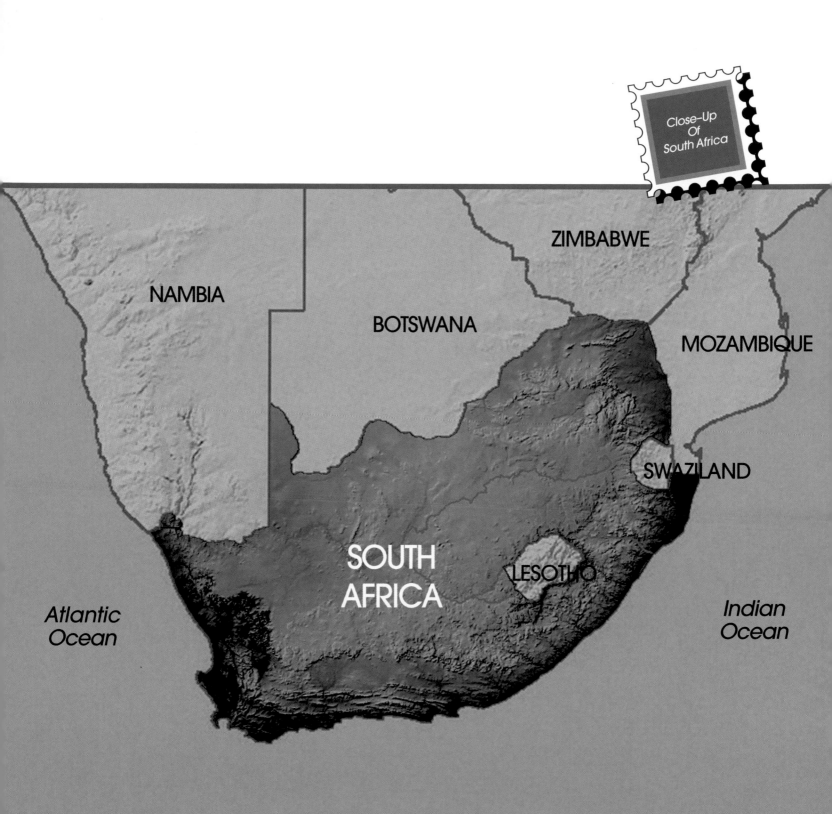

ZIMBABWE

NAMBIA

BOTSWANA

MOZAMBIQUE

SWAZILAND

SOUTH
AFRICA

LESOTHO

*Atlantic
Ocean*

*Indian
Ocean*

Close-Up
Of
South Africa

Table
Mountain
Near
Cape Town

Limpopo

Richtersveld
National
Park

Orange

Vaal

Lotent
Natural
Reserve

Orange

DRAKENSBERG MTS.

Cape Town

Table Mountain

Bob Krist/Corbis

The Land

Drakensberg Mountain

ABPL/Corbis

The countryside of South Africa is made up of flat sections of land called plateaus. South Africa's plateau area is surrounded by mountains called the Great Escarpment. The highest mountain in South Africa is called Champagne Castle.

South Africa sometimes doesn't get enough rain. Because of this, there are very few rivers. The three major rivers are the Orange, the Vaal, and the Limpopo. The Orange River is the longest. It is 1,330 miles long!

ABPL/Corbis

Valley In The Lotent Natural Reserve

Orange River In Richtersveld National Park

ABPL/Corbis

Leopard In Sabi Sands Private Reserve

Many rare animals live in South Africa. Elephants, lions, giraffes, zebras, and leopards all can be found there. Baboons, crocodiles, and snakes live in South Africa, too. Each year, thousands of people visit the great national parks where the animals are protected. The largest and most famous national park in South Africa is Kruger National Park.

There are also many rare plants and grasses in South Africa. For example, the cycad is a huge tropical plant that has been on this planet for a very long time. It can grow to be more than 150 feet tall!

Kevin Schafer/Corbis

Giraffe In Kruger National Park

Douglas Peebles/Corbis

Natal Cycad Plant

Darrell Gulin/Corbis

TRANSVAAL

Kruger
National
Park

Sabi Sands
Private
Reserve

NATAL

Elephants
In Eastern
Transvaal

British Ambassadors
During 1879
Zulu War

Mafeking

ZULULAND

Hulton-Deutsch Collection/Corbis

Zulu King, Cetewayo, In 1870 Zululand

Hulton-Deutsch Collection/Corbis

The first people in South Africa lived on the grasslands in small groups called tribes. The tribes lived off of the land and were very happy. Then about 300 years ago, people from the country of Europe started arriving in South Africa. At first the African tribes and their new neighbors got along. But slowly, the Europeans and the Africans began to fight over the land. These small battles soon led to wars between the Europeans and the tribes.

In 1910, The Union of South Africa was formed. It was a government run only by white people. This government brought the country together, but it did not bring peace. Many people did not think it was fair that only white people could run the government.

Zulu Warriors Of 1888

Corbis-Bettmann

Soon, the government of South Africa set up a system called apartheid (uh–PAR–tite), which means "apart." Under apartheid, black people had to ride separate buses, eat in different restaurants, and use separate rest rooms. White and black children couldn't even play together. The people of South Africa wanted apartheid to change, but it took many years.

Boers In 1899 Battle At Mafeking

Hulton-Deutsch Collection/Corbis

Today, South Africa is led by an African man named Nelson Mandela. He is a brave man who spent 28 years in prison because he fought against apartheid. Nelson Mandela believed that a country should be governed by everyone, not just a few people. With his help, there is less fighting among the people about who should be in charge. Today in South Africa there is hope for peace.

Durban's City Hall

Dave G. Houser/Corbis

Business District In Cape Town

Neil Beer/Corbis

Capital Cities: ☆

☆ Pretoria

Bloemfontein ☆

• Durban

☆ Cape Town

Jacques M. Chenet/Corbis

Nelson
Mandela

A Rural African Home

North Cape

NATAL

TRANSKEI

Lindsay Hebberd/Corbis

Farm On North Cape At Desert's Edge

The years of apartheid were hard on the people of South Africa. While white people were able to buy fancy houses and nice clothes, black South Africans were poor. They had to live in the poor areas and work jobs that did not pay very much money. Today, this is changing. Without apartheid, black South Africans can get better jobs. They can buy nicer houses and newer clothes. For many people, South Africa is a much happier place—without apartheid.

ABPL/Corbis

Tony Arruza/Corbis

Hanging up Clothes In Transkei Village

Black Village in Natal

Nik Wheeler/Corbis

City Life And Country Life

South Africa's cities are very much like the cities in the United States. Tall buildings and busy streets are common sights. And some cities have parks and fountains, too! Just like in the United States, city people live in apartments or houses. They drive cars or ride buses to get from place to place.

Life in the country is a little different. Most black South Africans live in areas called homelands. There are ten homelands that are scattered like puzzle pieces across the country. One of these areas is called the KwaZulu-Natal.

Xhosa Village Homes In Transkei

Tony Arruza/Corbis

This is the homeland of the Zulu tribe. Here the Zulus farm and raise cows. They live in huts that are made from reeds and straw. There aren't any windows in the huts and the floor is made of packed dirt. A Zulu hut looks a lot like a beehive!

Tony Arruza/Corbis

City Of Cape Town

Village Stone Fences And Grass Huts

Lindsay Hebberd/Corbis

ABPL/Corbis

NATAL

• Pietermaritzburg

TRANSKEI

Cape Town

The City Of Pietermaritzburg In Natal

Teacher
Helping
Student

Pretoria

Johannesburg

NATAL

Port Elizabeth

Lindsay Hebberd/Corbis

In South Africa, children are taught to speak and read in more than one language. In the lower grades, many children learn in the language of their tribe. Then in the upper grades, many students learn English. They also learn a language called Afrikaans. With so many languages to learn, students in South Africa need to work hard. They also learn things such as math and science, just like you.

Classroom Studies In Natal Area

Lindsay Hebberd/Corbis

Students Outside School Near Johannesburg

Class Studying Agriculture Near Port Elizabeth

ABPL/Corbis

ABPL/Corbis

Work

For many years, South Africa was known as "the land of gold and diamonds." Many people worked in the country's mines to gather the sparkling stones. Today the people of South Africa have many other kinds of jobs. Factories in the cities produce machinery and clothes. South Africa also has many people who work in the fields. There they grow and harvest such things as sugar cane and wheat.

Harvesting Tea In Tzaneen

Photographex/© Corbis

Pietemaritzburg Factory

DeBeer's Diamond Mine Workers In 1901

Library of Congress/Corbis

Paul Almasy/© Corbis

ABPL/Corbis

Tzaneen

Diamond Mines

Pietermaritzburg

Cotton Belt

Women Picking Cotton

Ostrich Eggs From Oudtshoorn

Kruger National Park

Shakaland

Cape Town Oudtshoorn

Ground Nuts From Shakaland

Nik Wheeler/Corbis

Foods from many different countries have found a home in South Africa. The Dutch, the Greeks, the Germans, the Chinese, and the Indians have all added some of their cooking ideas to South African dishes.

A favorite food in South Africa is mealie, a meal in a bowl. Mealie is a porridge made with corn and milk. Many South Africans also like to eat ostrich eggs!

Cape Town Market Place

Canned Meat Processing Near Kruger National Park

ABPL/Corbis

Hans Georg Roth/Corbis

Pastimes

South Africans like to play sports such as rugby, cricket, and squash. But because of apartheid, for many years people from South Africa were not allowed to take part in games with other countries—like the Olympics. Thankfully, this has changed.

Women Play Lacrosse On Horseback In Pietermaritzburg

Nik Wheeler/Corbis

Cricket Match In Port Elizabeth

ABPL/Corbis

Today blacks and whites play together in South Africa. And together, they are champions. In 1992, South Africa sent a team to the Olympics for the first time in many years. In 1995, the country's soccer team won the All-African Cup. In South Africa, many sports help blacks and whites work together as a team.

Bob Krist/Corbis

Pietermaritzburg

Oudtshoorn • Port Eliizabeth

Ostrich
Racing
In
Oudtshoorn

Zulus Celebrate In Traditional Ways

ZULULAND

Wolfberg Arch
+
Cape Province

Nik Wheeler/Corbis

Vinyards Of Cape Province

ABPL/Corbis

Many South Africans celebrate Christmas and Easter. They also celebrate a special day called the Day of the Vow. On this day, many people honor those who died in a great battle between the Europeans and the Zulu tribe. Today, the Day of the Vow is a special day that reminds the people of South Africa to work together for peace.

ABPL/Corbis

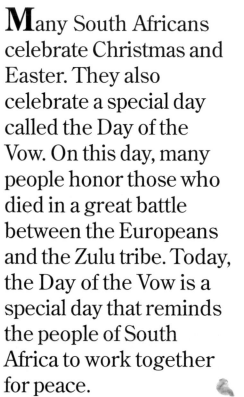

Unusual Wolfberg Arch

South Africa is a beautiful country with wonderful things to see. The special mix of people, animals, plants, and food makes South Africa a very interesting place to visit—and to live! Maybe one day, you will visit this special country, too.

Woman
Weaving
Tribal
Design

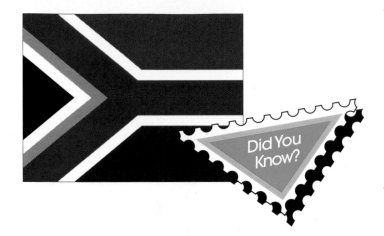

Did You Know?

South Africa is really called "The Republic of South Africa." People just say "South Africa" for short.

South Africa's main crops are corn, wheat, sugar, potatoes, tobacco, and fruit.

Wonderbooms are evergreen trees that grow in South Africa. They are also called Wondertrees.

The Zulu tribe of South Africa uses beads to communicate. They even write each other "love letters" with different patterns of red, white, and green beads.

How Do You Say?

	AFRIKAANS	*HOW TO SAY IT*
Hello	goeiemôre	KHOO–yuh–MORE–uh
Goodbye	tot siens	TOHT SEENZ
Please	asseblief	AHS–suh–BLEEF
Thank You	danke	DAHN–kee
One	een	EE–uhn
Two	twe	TWEE–uh
Three	drie	DREE
South Africa	Suid-Afrika	SITE AH–free–kuh

Glossary

apartheid (uh–PAR–tite)
Apartheid was a system that the old South African government used. Under apartheid, laws gave white people special rights over colored people.

continent (KON–tuh–nent)
Most of the land areas on Earth are divided up into huge sections called continents. South Africa is on the continent of Africa.

mealie (MEE–lee)
Mealie is a favorite food in South Africa. It is a porridge made of corn and milk.

plateau (pla–TOH)
A plateau is an area that is higher than the areas of land around it. South Africa's plateau is surrounded by mountains.

tribe (TRYB)
A tribe is a small group of people that lives together and has the same way of doing things. There are many different tribes in South Africa.

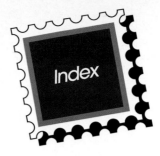

Index